# ENGINEERING SOLUTIONS FOR FLOODS AND TSUNAMIS

CORONA BREZINA

New York

Published in 2020 by The Rosen Publishing Group, Inc.
29 East 21st Street, New York, NY 10010



First Edition



**Library of Congress Cataloging-in-Publication Data**

Names: Brezina, Corona, author.
Title: Engineering solutions for floods and tsunamis / Corona Brezina.
Description: First edition. | New York: Rosen Publishing, 2020. | Series: Preparing for disaster | Includes bibliographical references and index.
Identifiers: LCCN 2019009436| ISBN 9781725347823 (library bound) | ISBN 9781725347816 (pbk.)
Subjects: LCSH: Emergency management—Juvenile literature. | Hazard mitigation—Juvenile literature. | Floods—Juvenile literature. | Tsunamis—Juvenile literature.
Classification: LCC HD49 .B74 2020 | DDC 627/.4—dc23
LC record available at https://lccn.loc.gov/2019009436

*Manufactured in the United States of America*

# CONTENTS

# Introduction

Floods and tsunamis are natural disasters that can inflict destruction on lives, property, ecosystems, and world economies. Human beings cannot prevent floods or tsunamis, but it is possible to be thoroughly prepared when disaster strikes.

Science, technology, engineering, and mathematics—the STEM fields—provide tools to predict floods and tsunamis and mitigate, or reduce, their damage. A number of different kinds of scientists study the weather, water, and Earth's natural processes. Meteorologists study and predict the weather and climate. Hydrologists study the properties and movement of water on and under Earth's surface and in the atmosphere. Geologists study rocks and the other substances that make up Earth. Oceanographers study properties of the ocean.

Engineers from many different fields design and build solutions that protect people and property from floods and tsunamis. They construct levees and dams. They make the instruments that detect and monitor floods and tsunamis. They create the communication networks that keep authorities and the public informed when disaster strikes. Cutting-edge technology and mathematics are essential to creating computer models of floods and tsunamis and developing innovative new methods of preventing damage.

Disaster management authorities aim to mitigate flood and tsunami risk. Mitigation means reducing the likelihood of damage to people and property when disaster strikes.

After Hurricane Katrina caused massive flooding in 2005, New Orleans constructed new defenses, including the Gulf Intracoastal Waterway West Closure Complex. The complex is the world's largest drainage pump system.

Instruments that predict or detect floods and tsunamis give emergency planners time to prepare in advance. Communication systems enable people to leave their homes before the water arrives. Engineering projects direct the water away from buildings and infrastructure. Individual preparedness measures, such as safeguarding homes and belongings against flooding, can reduce loss of personal possessions. Government agencies, local communities, humanitarian organizations, and individuals can all contribute to emergency preparedness measures based on STEM principles that can mitigate the damage done by floods and tsunamis.

CHAPTER ONE

# The Science of Fierce Floods and Terrible Tsunamis

Floods and tsunamis are natural disasters caused by the power of water. A flood occurs when land that is usually dry is temporarily covered by water. Tsunamis are huge, long waves that rush toward coastlines from the ocean. Both floods and tsunamis can cause catastrophic damage.

## What Happens During Floods

Floods happen in all fifty states and all of the US territories. According to the National Severe Storms Laboratory, floods are the most common and widespread type of natural disaster related to weather.

Many floods are caused by weather events. Storms, hurricanes, and cyclones can lead to flooding. Rising water levels that occur during a storm are called a storm surge. Storm surges mainly affect the coasts. Floods can also be caused by other natural events. High tides can cause floods. So can melting snow and ice. Other natural disasters can trigger floods, too. Examples include earthquakes, tsunamis, and landslides.

Human activities can cause some floods. Engineers can intentionally cause a flood by releasing water controlled by dams. They may flood an area to provide water for farming or to help the environment. The catastrophic failure of dams or other man-made structures built to control water can sometimes create floods as well.

In 2011, an earthquake triggered a tsunami that struck the coast of Japan. The event caused flooding and other consequences, such as fires and damage to a nuclear power plant.

Floods often occur when a river or stream overflows its banks. The level at which it goes over is called flood stage. The water rises to cover the surrounding land. This area, which is dry most of the time, is called the floodplain.

Floods can occur slowly or quickly. Sometimes, water rises gradually over many days or even weeks. Other times, water rushes in rapidly. When this rapid rush happens, it is called a flash flood. Flash floods are very dangerous. They cannot always be predicted, and the arrival of water can catch people by surprise.

Certain areas are at high risk for flash floods. These include densely populated urban areas and land surrounding rivers. Runoff from mountains can cause flash floods. Canyons and dry riverbeds in the West can rapidly fill with water after a heavy rain. In the spring, rain combined with melting snow and ice can produce flash floods.

A flood can affect a small area, such as a neighborhood in a city. Or it can cover a huge region, sometimes across multiple states.

Floods can be good for the land. The water spreads around mud and silt. The nutrients left behind by flooding can benefit farming.

But floods also cause great destruction. People can drown during floods or be killed by the hazards that accompany flooding. Floods wash away soil and destroy crops. Rushing water can carry away cars, trees, and structures. Infrastructure such as roads and bridges is damaged. Power outages and gas leaks may occur.

The destruction caused by floods continues to cause problems long after the water recedes. Immediately after a flood, the water may be unsafe to drink. Chemicals or sewage can contaminate the water. Drinking unsafe water can spread disease.

When people return to their homes, they may find that their belongings have been damaged or destroyed by water. Floods can undermine and crack the foundations of houses. Harmful mold and mildew can grow on walls, furniture, and other possessions. Communities must dispose of debris. If flooding destroyed crops, food prices may rise afterward.

Cleaning up and rebuilding after a flood can be very expensive. Every year, floods cause billions of dollars' worth of damage in the United States. In 2011, for example, a record Mississippi River flood caused $2.8 billion in damages, according to the Army Corps of Engineers.

Residents attempt to salvage belongings from their flooded home in Houston, Texas. In 2017, heavy rains caused by Hurricane Harvey flooded a third of the city.

## What Happens During Tsunamis

People often picture a tsunami as a single, huge wave. That's only partially correct. Tsunamis are enormous. But a tsunami is actually a series of waves. They are all produced by the same trigger event.

## The 2004 Indian Ocean Tsunami

On December 26, 2004, an earthquake triggered the deadliest tsunami in recorded history. The quake was later determined to be the third most powerful ever measured. It struck off the coast of the island nation of Indonesia, which is in the Indian and Pacific Oceans. A huge tsunami was produced that traveled outward in all directions. About half an hour later, the first massive wave struck the Indonesian island of Sumatra.

Fourteen countries in Asia and Africa were affected by the tsunami. The worst damage occurred on the Indonesian islands, where waves over 100 feet (30 meters) in height rushed onto the coasts. According to Timothy Kusky, a professor of earth sciences and an author of a book on tsunamis, in total, more than 280,000 people lost their lives. About 1.7 million people were made homeless. Many more people died as a result of disease in the aftermath.

Tsunamis are caused by disturbances to the seafloor. Earthquakes are the most common cause of tsunamis. In general, more powerful earthquakes produce more destructive tsunamis. The most powerful earthquake ever measured occurred in 1960 near Chile. It produced a huge tsunami that devastated Chile and reached Hawaii, Japan, and the Philippines.

Not all underwater earthquakes cause tsunamis, however. Most earthquakes occur along fault lines where tectonic plates meet. Tectonic plates are the big plates of solid rock that make up Earth's outer layer. The plates are continuously moving, either toward, past, or away from one another. Tsunamis are most likely to occur when the earthquake creates a big change in the ocean's floor height between two plates. The uplifted floor causes a huge disturbance in the water as the water is displaced.

Erupting volcanoes can also cause tsunamis. Volcanoes have produced some of the biggest known tsunamis. Sometimes, the force of an underwater eruption can trigger a tsunami. In other cases, the tsunami occurs when the erupting volcano collapses. In 1883, for example, the volcano Krakatau in Indonesia collapsed after erupting. A huge hole was formed. Ocean water rushed in, producing a series of tsunamis. Volcanic eruptions sometimes occur along with earthquakes.

Landslides can cause tsunamis as well. These landslides may occur on land. In 1958, an earthquake in Alaska caused an enormous landslide that triggered a tsunami, for example. Or the landslide can happen underwater. Sometimes an erupting volcano causes a landslide. A deep-sea landslide can be triggered by an earthquake, too.

Some scientists think that it is possible for a tsunami to result from an asteroid hitting the ocean. But it is very unlikely that an asteroid strike would produce a hugely destructive tsunami.

Tsunamis can be enormous. Some of the biggest have been more than 100 feet (30 m) high, according to the National Oceanic and Atmospheric Administration (NOAA). Most waves travel on the top of the ocean. But tsunamis extend through the entire depth of water in the ocean. They also travel very fast in the ocean. NOAA also reports that they can go over 500 miles per hour (800 kilometers per hour). A tsunami slows when it reaches shallow water close to land. Then it travels only at 20 to 30 miles per hour (32–48 kmh). But the tsunami grows taller and stronger as it nears the coast.

If a tsunami is triggered close to land, the wave could arrive within minutes. Tsunamis that travel greater distances may travel for many hours.

People sometimes say that an approaching tsunami looks like a wall of water and that the wave sounds like the roar of a train. Smaller tsunamis rush in like a sudden flood. Water from a tsunami can surge up rivers and cover low-lying land. The Chilean tsunami carried wreckage of houses a couple miles inland.

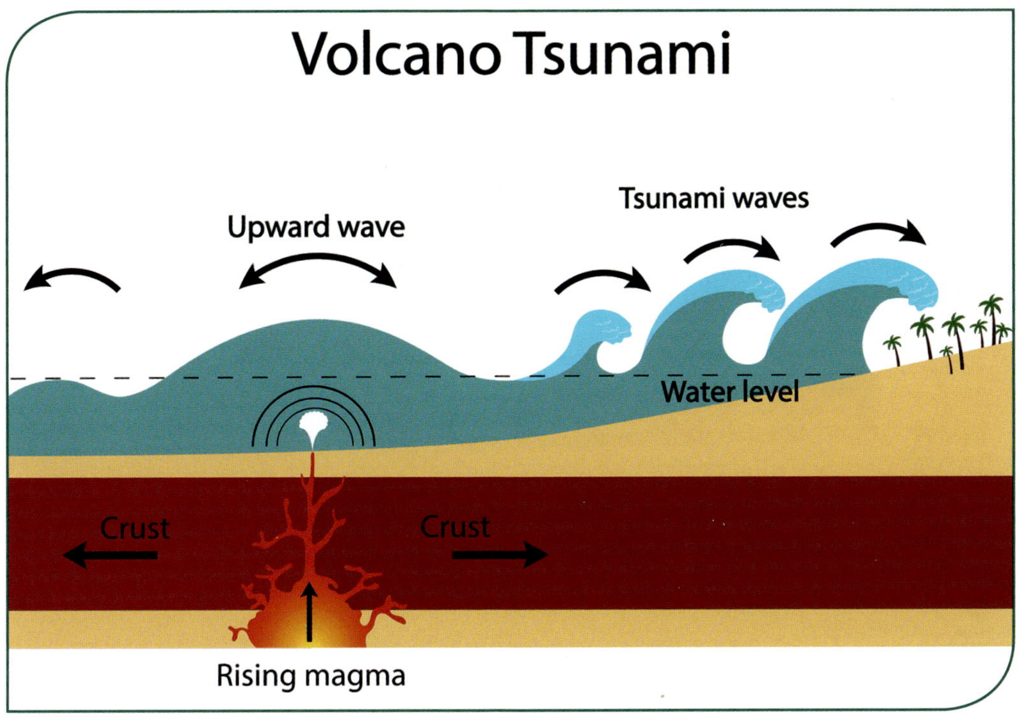


This diagram shows how an erupting underwater volcano triggers a tsunami. Waves are caused by the displacement of water by the eruption.

Additional tsunami waves arrive in as little as five minutes or as long as two hours. Sometimes, the later waves are bigger than the first one. It's impossible to predict the total number of waves.

Tsunamis can be much more powerful than ordinary floods. People and debris can be caught up in the moving water and then pulled back into the ocean when the wave recedes. As with flooding, tsunamis cause damage to property and infrastructure.

CHAPTER TWO

# Flood Forecasting and Reducing Flood Damage

Floods can occur on coasts, near rivers, in cities, and in the mountains. Floods can be fast or slow. But for all types of floods, there are systems in place to handle them. Meteorologists predict floods ahead of time. Scientists and engineers study floods and mitigate the damage. Disaster management authorities deal with the effects of flooding.

## Before the Flood

If there is danger of a flood occurring, the National Weather Service (NWS) issues warnings to the public. Such weather alerts apply to specific areas. When the notification is displayed on a screen, it is often accompanied by a weather map that shows the affected areas.

A flood watch or flood advisory means that flooding is possible. A flood warning or flash flood warning means that flooding is certain to occur. Either it's already happening in some places or it's predicted to occur very soon.

Forecasting floods can be challenging. There are a lot of factors that contribute to flooding. Some floods may be predicted days or even weeks in advance. Others arrive quickly.

Experts such as meteorologists and hydrologists look at many different kinds of data to predict a flood. Real-time measurements allow them to track weather events as they're occurring. For instance, forecasters can monitor rainfall and river levels.

Tools such as radar enable forecasters to track storms. They can see the size of the storm and watch where it's raining the hardest. Satellites orbiting Earth also help predict and monitor floods. Satellite images show rainfall and the movement of water across the land.

Forecasters also need to know about ground conditions to predict flooding in an area. Factors include soil moisture and the shape of the land. The area may be paved over or covered by plants.

Computer models use this data to predict the chances of a flood. When water levels reach flood stage, the NWS categorizes the flood as minor, moderate, or major. A minor flood produces little damage. A major flood swamps roads and buildings.

Scientists use data to determine the long-term likelihood of floods in an area, too. They measure the flow of water in rivers. Then they use statistics to calculate the likelihood of flooding in surrounding areas. On a one-hundred-year floodplain, for example, a flood is expected to happen every hundred years, on average.

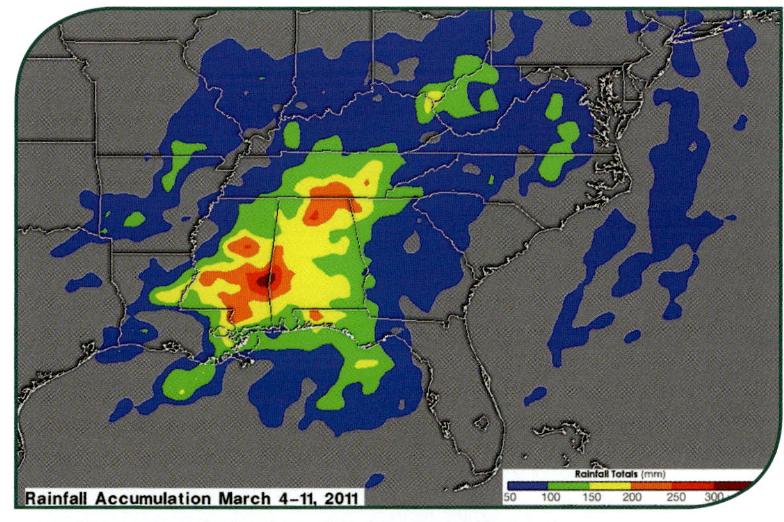


A National Aeronautics and Space Administration (NASA) weather map that uses satellite data displays the rainfall accumulation from a massive 2011 storm.

But that does not mean that floods occur exactly a hundred years apart. The "one-hundred-year flood" is just a statistical likelihood. It means that there is a

1 percent chance each year of a flood occurring in an area. In reality, one-hundred-year floods can happen more than every hundred years.

Planners use floodplain statistics in managing how land is used. There might be building restrictions on a one-hundred-year floodplain. But on a five-hundred-year floodplain, the risk of flooding isn't as high.

## Safeguarding Against Floods

Since ancient times, human beings have attempted to build structures to hold back floods. Today, people recognize that it's impossible to prevent flooding completely. Barricades such as dams and levees are still important for containing rising water. But other strategies can also mitigate damage from flooding.

Dams are structures built across a river to block or control the flow of water. The water is collected upstream from the dam in a reservoir—an artificial lake. Most dams are multipurpose. Water in a reservoir may be used for farming. Many dams produce electricity, too. But flood control is an important purpose for dams. When there's heavy rainfall or other flood triggers, the water fills the reservoir instead of flowing onto a floodplain. For example, two reservoirs protect the city of Houston, Texas. One of the reservoirs overflowed in 2017, after Hurricane Harvey caused heavy rainfall.

Levees are natural or artificial walls that contain the flow of water. Levees are often built on riverbanks. They are high enough to prevent water from spilling onto land during a flood. Many levees are constructed of soil and planted with grass to prevent erosion. Sometimes they are strengthened with concrete or other man-made materials.

Dams and levees are usually constructed as part of a larger water management system. Floodgates are sometimes built into water control structures. Floodgates can be opened and closed to release or contain water. In Maryland, for example, in 2011, Tropical Storm Lee caused the Susquehanna River to flood. Officials opened floodgates at the Conowingo Dam and ordered local residents to evacuate.

Water rushes from the floodgates of the Conowingo Dam in Port Deposit, Maryland, on September 8, 2011. The dam's fifty-three flood control gates can be opened when water levels rise.

Various kinds of channels and drainage structures can divert floodwaters away from buildings and communities. Spillways are passages built around dams or levees. If water threatens to overflow, spillways redirect it. Often, the water is released into a river. Floodways include waterways and portions of the floodplain that carry away floodwater. Water channels can sometimes be modified or created. Rivers can be altered so that they can carry more floodwater. Canals are man-made waterways used for many purposes. Some canals can help manage floodwater, such as the canal system in southern Florida. Culverts, or buried pipes, can direct water beneath roads or into canals.

Some floods are so strong that they can overwhelm flood control measures. Nonstructural flood mitigation measures are very important, too. Natural habitats can lessen the effects of floods. Wetlands, in particular, can absorb floodwater. Wetlands are areas that are covered by shallow water for at least part of the year. If wetlands are destroyed, floodwater might swamp areas occupied by people instead. On coasts, wetlands can defend against storm surges. Other natural features such as sand dunes can also provide protection.

Experts often recommend limiting development in areas likely to flood. Development is the construction of new buildings and infrastructure. Roads and houses and other structures built on a floodplain, for example, are vulnerable to flooding. The development can affect land away from the floodplain, too. If the floodplain is

This climate resilient home is being built to withstand extreme weather such as hurricanes and flooding.

altered, the water could be diverted to other places.

Construction methods can reduce a building's vulnerability to flooding. Houses can be elevated above flood level. They can be built out of materials that aren't likely to be damaged in case of a flood. Examples of flood-resistant structural materials include concrete, stone, steel, glass, brick, and treated lumber. Builders use brick or ceramic tile for walls, and slate, rubber, or plastic lumber for floors. They also make use of metal for doors and cabinets.

## Disaster Management and Floods

In the United States, the Army Corps of Engineers is the primary authority in charge of flood prevention and mitigation. The Federal Emergency Management Agency (FEMA) prepares for and responds to floods and other disasters. Other federal government departments are involved with understanding flood risk and determining policy, too.

Local and state governments also study dangers related to floods. They make laws and regulations that will protect people and property from flood damage. These rules may restrict development. Building codes may ensure that new structures can withstand flooding.

Planners in all levels of government also develop emergency preparedness measures in cases of disasters such as floods. Maps created by FEMA show whether an area is at risk of floods. In addition to NWS alerts, some communities send out texts or emails in case of an emergency. If a flood is predicted, the authorities may

## The Mississippi River Flood of 1927

The Mississippi River Flood of 1927 was the most destructive flood in the history of the United States. Heavy rains began to swell the river in the fall of 1926 and continued into 1927. In April, the system of levees began to collapse. The resulting flood covered 26,000 square miles (67,000 square kilometers) of land. Parts of Illinois, Missouri, Kentucky, Tennessee, Arkansas, Mississippi, and Louisiana were underwater. Five hundred people died in the floods and six hundred thousand lost their homes, according to *Time*.

The flood prompted reform to US flood policy. After the flood, the US government took on more responsibility for flood prevention. The Flood Control Act of 1928 approved a massive system of levees, floodways, dams, and other flood control measures on the Mississippi. The flood also affected how Americans obtained flood insurance. In 1928, private insurance companies stopped selling flood insurance. Eventually, in 1968, the National Flood Insurance Program (NFIP) was created. NFIP is managed by the Federal Emergency Management Agency.

order an evacuation. Everybody must leave their homes for their own safety. Organizations such as the American Red Cross provide shelter during emergencies.

After the water retreats, communities must clean up and repair the damage. Sometimes, extensive rebuilding is necessary. After a catastrophic flood, communities may adopt new rules to reduce flood risk in the future. In 2018, following Hurricane Harvey, for example, Houston passed rules requiring new construction in floodplains be built 2 feet (0.6 m) above the level of a five-hundred-year flood.

# CHAPTER THREE

# Tracking Tsunamis

Tsunamis are impossible to predict. There is no tsunami season. The triggers that cause tsunamis often occur without warning. But scientists and engineers can prepare for the possibility of a tsunami. They detect and monitor events that could produce tsunamis. Once a tsunami is observed, emergency alerts are issued.

## Detecting Tsunamis

Tsunamis are monitored by two tsunami warning centers, run by NOAA. There is the National Tsunami Warning Center and the Pacific Tsunami Warning Center.

One of the tsunami warning centers' most important jobs is to make observations. The centers monitor instrument readings from around the world. This monitoring includes seismic and water level networks. The seismic network tracks earthquake activity. The tsunami warning centers analyze information about earthquakes, such as location and strength. The waves produced by earthquakes travel much faster than tsunamis. Therefore, instruments detect earthquakes ahead of tsunamis.

Tsunamis caused by landslides and volcanoes are harder to detect and forecast. But they are also rarer than tsunamis produced by earthquakes.

If scientists at the centers believe that an earthquake could possibly trigger a tsunami, they examine data from water-level networks. Monitors called deep-ocean assessment and reporting of tsunami (DART) systems report information about conditions on the open ocean. A DART system is made up of an instrument attached to the ocean floor linked to a buoy on the surface. Scientists analyze DART system measurements to learn more about an approaching tsunami.

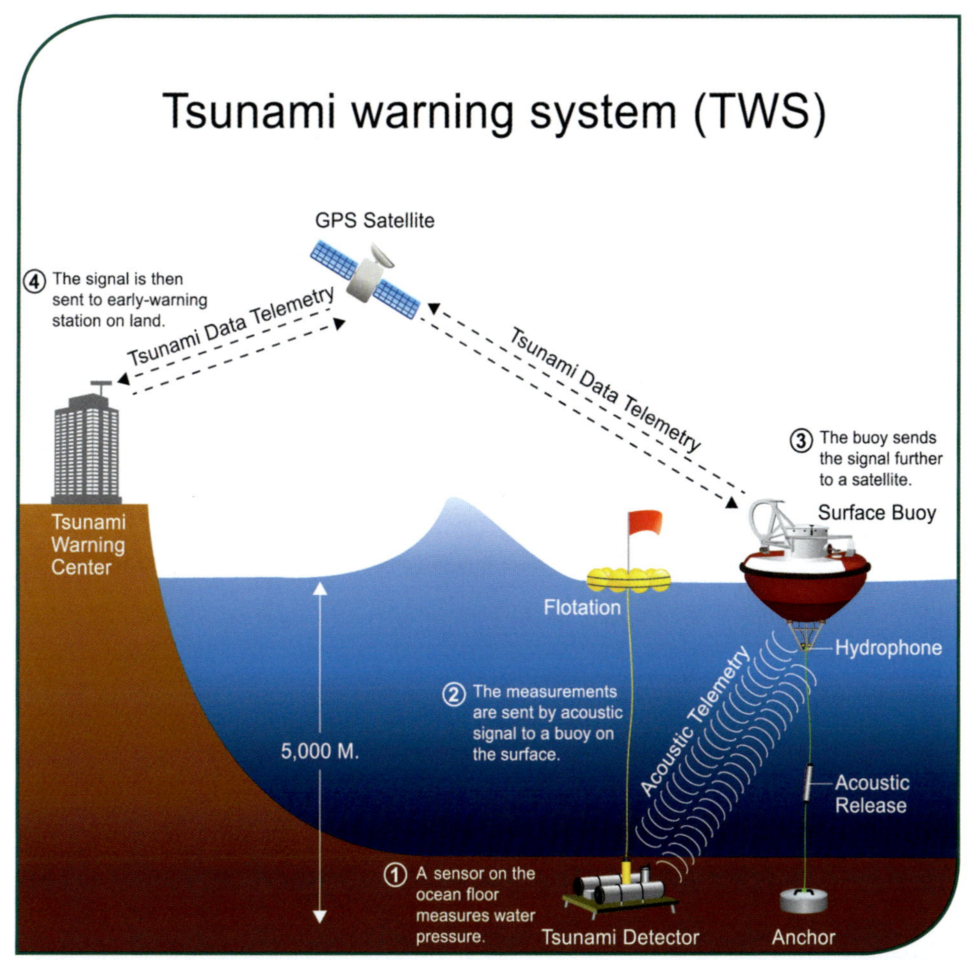


A diagram of a tsunami warning system shows the sensors, buoys, and communication systems that alert scientists about an approaching tsunami.

Dozens of DART systems monitor activity in the Pacific and Atlantic Oceans, the Gulf of Mexico, and the Caribbean Sea. The US system is linked to a bigger worldwide network.

Coastal water-level stations also report data that can help predict tsunamis. These stations are located close to land. They mostly monitor ocean tides. But coastal water-level stations also collect valuable information about a tsunami's size and the time it arrives.

Scientists enter data about seismic activity and changes in water level into forecast models. The models also use information about past tsunamis and earthquakes. The models produce a forecast about the tsunami's path. A tsunami travels outward in all directions from its starting point. The forecast predicts which places the tsunami will hit and how much flooding will occur. It predicts the size of the waves and the arrival time. The centers advise communities as to how long they will be in danger from the tsunami.

## Recognizing Signs of an Approaching Tsunami

Official agencies issue tsunami warnings as soon as a tsunami is detected. They also recommend that people be aware of natural tsunami warnings. If you're near the ocean on a coast at high risk for tsunamis, unusual activity occurring in the water or on the beach could indicate an approaching tsunami. The beach might start shaking. The water could drain away quickly, revealing a long stretch of ocean floor. You might see the tsunami approaching in the distance. If any of these events occur, immediately move to higher ground. Avoid rivers—the tsunami can travel up them and overflow their banks. Remain on high ground until all of the waves have hit and the authorities announce that it's safe to return.

As the tsunami travels closer to land, scientists receive fresh data. They update the forecast to provide more precise information to the public.

## Tsunami Readiness

When there is an event that could cause a tsunami, the tsunami warning centers release statements with information. They send out messages even if a tsunami is not expected. Officials want to reassure authorities that they're monitoring the situation.

If a tsunami is possible, the centers send out alerts. The alert includes the threat level and specific information about the event. A tsunami watch means that a tsunami is possible in the area where it is issued. A tsunami advisory is sent out when a tsunami is expected to affect the area, but not to cause much damage. Strong currents and waves may arrive. Local officials may be advised to close beaches and evacuate harbors.

A tsunami warning alerts the public that a dangerous tsunami is predicted. Tsunami warnings are spread on TV, radio, and official websites. Some communities warn residents through text and telephone alert systems. Outdoor sirens may sound.

Local officials may order evacuations of low-lying areas. They may close roads. Boats in harbors are at risk. Officials may advise that boats be moved to deeper waters if there's time.

Tsunamis are more dangerous when they are generated close to the coast. These local tsunamis can arrive within minutes. People have little time to prepare or evacuate.

A tsunami could hit any US coastline. But some areas are at higher risk than others. The risk is greatest for the coastlines of the western states, Alaska, and Hawaii. The Caribbean and Pacific islands are also at high risk. Low-lying areas are in the most danger. Tsunami risk is low on the Atlantic Coast and Gulf Coast.

Residents in high-risk states can check maps to learn more about the risk in their area. These tsunami inundation maps are available through the National Tsunami Hazard Mitigation Program (NTHMP). High-tech computer models are used to make tsunami inundation maps. They consider factors such as location, geological data, and historical records of past tsunamis. The online versions have interactive features. Emergency planners consult these maps for tsunami preparedness.

Barricades such as seawalls can be built along the coast to shield land from tsunamis. Natural barriers can also provide protection. Examples include coastal forests, reefs, and sand dunes. After the 2004 tsunami, for example, parts of the Sri Lankan coast with these natural features were not damaged as badly as developed areas.

In 2012, Hurricane Sandy destroyed boardwalks on vulnerable coasts. A year after the storm, sandbags and artificial sand dunes protected a section of New York coastline.

## Disaster Management and Tsunamis

NOAA is the federal agency responsible for preventing tsunami disasters. Its responsibilities go beyond detecting tsunamis and issuing warnings. NOAA educates the public about tsunamis. NOAA scientists perform research on tsunamis. The agency also works with other federal, state, and local groups on tsunami readiness.

The US Geological Survey (USGS) runs the seismic network

that monitors earthquakes. It monitors volcanoes and landslides. The agency also performs tsunami research and models hazards that trigger tsunamis.

A sign marks a tsunami evacuation route on the island of Ko Phi Phi Leh, Thailand. The island was devastated by the Indian Ocean tsunami in 2004.

FEMA works to reduce the risk of possible natural disasters, including tsunamis. When tsunamis do strike, FEMA responds with relief efforts. The agency also keeps the public updated when tsunamis and other natural disasters occur.

Public education is essential to preventing loss of life when a tsunami strikes. Residents may not have much time to prepare for an evacuation. People must know ahead of time what to do if there's a tsunami warning. They should be familiar with the community's emergency plan. Everyone should know evacuation routes in case of a tsunami. Officials should be prepared to assist the public. Communities can prepare for tsunamis through the TsunamiReady program, created by the NWS and the NTHMP.

Most tsunamis are small. They cause little damage. But the worst tsunamis cause catastrophic destruction. Effective warning systems and solid emergency preparedness can save lives.

CHAPTER FOUR

# Promising Solutions

The twenty-first century has seen many advances in predicting floods and tsunamis and mitigating their effects. But dealing with floods and tsunamis will continue to be an ongoing effort. Forecasters have to consider many different factors in predicting floods and tsunamis. Emergency planners also deal with complex situations. In the future, their jobs could get even more complicated.

## Looking Ahead

Some experts believe that climate change will make the effects of flooding and tsunamis worse. And the world's population is increasing. More people will be affected by natural disasters such as floods and hurricanes in the coming years and decades.

One of the effects of climate change is rising ocean levels. Communities on the coasts will have to take steps to prevent and mitigate flooding. Many big cities are located on coasts. According to the National Ocean Service, 39 percent of the US population lived on the coasts in 2010. That number is 123.3 million people.

Many coastal communities in the United States are already seeing frequent, severe flooding. Sometimes, people move away to escape the floods. In other places, cities have approved measures to fight flooding. In Miami Beach, Florida, for example, city streets often flood at high tide. In 2017, the city began a big project to raise roads, put in pumps, add main lines in water supply systems, and revamp sewer connections.

After New Orleans flooded in 2005 during Hurricane Katrina, engineers installed a powerful new set of pumps close to the site where levees failed.

Climate change is also changing weather patterns. Periods of heavy rainfall are expected to become even more intense. According to the Environmental Protection Agency, the one-hundred-year floodplain is expected to grow by 45 percent by 2100.

Hurricanes are also becoming more destructive because of climate change. The combination of rising ocean levels and stronger storms could bring a greater number of catastrophic floods to the coasts in the future. Coastal communities will be more vulnerable to storm surges. Higher ocean levels will also allow tsunamis to reach farther inland.

Climate change is predicted to worsen the effects of other natural disasters, too. Wildfires have been becoming bigger, for example. Areas that have been burned by wildfire are at a high risk for flooding. The ground cannot absorb much water. Even moderate rainfall can cause flash floods in areas that have been burned by wildfires. The floodwater carries soil and debris, too. Flooding can create mudslides and debris flows, as occurred in Southern California in early 2019.

According to FEMA, property below burn areas may be at higher risk of flooding for five years after the wildfire. Homeowners should strengthen their houses against flooding. Experts recommend that when communities rebuild after wildfires, they take steps to reduce risk in case of future fires. These steps can include building with fire-resistant materials and ensuring that dead shrubs and brush in yards are removed.

Population growth is also a factor in planning for future floods. More people will be living along the coasts. They will be vulnerable to tsunamis and coastal flooding. There will also be more people living in cities. Densely populated areas are vulnerable to flash flooding. During a heavy rainfall, rain flows off of pavement and roofs. There is not enough bare ground to absorb water. Storm drains can overflow, resulting in flooding.

Cities of the future will need to engineer solutions to flooding. Innovations include permeable pavement, for example, which allows rainfall to drain through it to reduce runoff. It can be used for driveways, sidewalks, and parking lots. Restored wetlands could be incorporated into communities, too.

Water is being sprayed on a permeable pavement project during Earth Week in California to demonstrate the material's drainage capabilities.

## Learning from Experience

Because of their geography, certain countries have had to develop extensive protections against floods or tsunamis. The Netherlands, for example, is a low-lying country in Europe. Two-thirds of its land is prone to flooding. A third lies below sea level. The Netherlands has been battling to hold back the water for more than a thousand years. In the thirteenth century, the Dutch

## The 2011 Earthquake and Tsunami

On March 11, 2011, a huge earthquake occurred off the coast of Japan. The Great East Japan Earthquake, as it's now called, was the fourth most powerful earthquake ever detected. It triggered a huge tsunami. Within an hour, the first waves struck Japan's coast, surging inland and causing massive destruction. The largest waves were 128 feet (39 m) high, according to LiveScience. Nearly twenty thousand people lost their lives in the disaster, most of them swept away by the tsunami. The water also damaged the Fukushima Daiichi Nuclear Power Plant, causing a nuclear emergency.

The effects of the disasters were felt worldwide. The powerful earthquake altered the rotation of Earth. Smaller tsunamis triggered by the quake hit Alaska, Hawaii, and Chile. For years afterward, debris from the tsunami washed up on beaches in Canada and the United States.

The recovery costs of the disaster were estimated at $235 billion by the World Bank. By contrast, total costs of tsunami damage in the United States since the beginning of the twentieth century is less than $2 billion, according to NOAA.

began building a system of dikes—barriers to protect against flooding. By the fifteenth century, they were using windmills to pump away water.

In 1953, however, a catastrophic flood struck the country. Dikes broke and more than 1,800 people died, according to Chris Iovenko in *EARTH Magazine*. The Dutch launched an ambitious new effort to hold back the water. They built a huge engineering project called Delta Works. It consisted of a system of dams, dikes, and sea gates. The project was a success. Nobody has died from flooding in the Netherlands since 1953.

But in the 1990s, two huge floods occurred once again across the country. The Dutch started to worry about the possibility of rising sea levels. They began engineering new approaches to controlling the water.

One of the resulting projects is called Room for the River, which was launched in 2006. Instead of building more barriers, Room for the River gives the water more space. Rivers were widened. Floodplains were restored. Some of the dikes were reduced. With this new project, the Dutch believe that they will be able to adapt to the consequences of climate change.

The Dutch are widely viewed as the world's experts in managing water. When countries experience catastrophic floods, they often consult

The new channels and expanded floodplains of the IJssel River in the Netherlands allow more space for overflow, part of the Room for the River project.

with Dutch engineers on how to recover. The Dutch strongly encourage prevention measures. According to the Dutch view, money is better spent on flood protection than on recovery measures after disaster strikes.

Japan is an island nation prone to frequent earthquakes. The country is at high risk for tsunamis, too. The word "tsunami" comes from the Japanese language.

Japan set up a tsunami warning system in 1952. The country also has one of the world's most advanced earthquake monitoring systems. The damage and death toll from the 2011 tsunami would have been much greater if Japan had not been prepared for disaster.

The earthquake and tsunami were too huge for the monitoring systems to handle, however. After the earthquake was detected, a tsunami alert was quickly issued. But the prediction of the size was low. Seawalls and sea gates protected many communities on the coast. But they were not tall enough to stop the waves.

Japan has learned from the 2011 disaster and improved its tsunami preparedness. The seismic system has been expanded. The country increased the number of land-based seismic sensors and motion meters. It also improved power and satellite communications. Japan's government has expanded its tsunami text notification and public alert system. New detection instruments will be able to handle a "megaquake" like the 2011 event. Several DART systems have been installed to monitor tsunamis in the ocean. Huge seawalls have been built along the coasts, and construction in some low-lying coastal areas is restricted. Japan continues to explore innovative approaches that could improve tsunami predictions in the future.

CHAPTER FIVE

# Be Prepared! What You Can Do

People should be aware of the dangers of floods and tsunamis. Education and preparedness are essential. Individuals should know the risk of floods and tsunamis in their area. They should be familiar with city emergency plans. Families should also have personal emergency plans in place. Homeowners can also take steps to protect their homes and property.

## Know the Danger

FEMA and other government agencies can provide maps and resources so that residents can be informed about flood and tsunami risk in their area. Homeowners should research flood risk before buying a house. Renters should consider their risk as well, especially if they live at ground level or store belongings in a basement.

Homeowners who live in high-risk areas should buy flood insurance. Most home insurance policies do not pay for flood damage. The National Flood Insurance Program (NFIP) offers insurance that covers flooding, including from tsunamis. It's available to homeowners, renters, and business owners. People who live in areas that have been affected by wildfires may also qualify for flood insurance.

Residents of the coastal town of Seaside Heights, New Jersey, begin to rebuild a year after Hurricane Sandy caused widespread destruction in 2012. Rebuilding codes included improved flood resistant construction methods.

Residents should take steps to make their homes and property safe in case of a flood or tsunami. If a basement tends to flood, appliances and electrical systems should be removed or elevated. Valuable possessions should be stored on higher levels. Homeowners should consider waterproofing basements, which can range from applying sealant to installing a drainage system. Pumps and water-alarm systems are available in case of flooding. Owners who are building new homes in high-risk areas should elevate the structures above flood levels.

People should support flood mitigation measures in their communities. Flood risk should be considered in planning new developments. Green areas should be preserved. Wetlands are particularly effective in mitigating flood risk.

Environmentally friendly measures to reduce flood risk can benefit a community. Rain gardens, for example, collect water during heavy rains. Rain gardens are attractive, too. They can be planted in parks. Or people can create small rain gardens in their yards.

## Have an Emergency Plan

Residents should take action to protect their property and well-being before disaster strikes. Families should keep an emergency kit handy. It should contain food, water, a first aid kit, a cell phone, and other supplies. The government website Ready.gov offers tips on items to

## Beware the Water

Moving water is very dangerous during floods and tsunamis. You may think that it's safe to walk across a shallow stretch of floodwater. But according to FEMA, water that is just 6 inches (15 centimeters) deep can knock a person down if the current is strong. The water could be contaminated with gasoline or sewage as well. You could also be injured by debris.

If you're evacuating by car, never drive through floodwater. The water might be deeper than it looks. A foot of floodwater can carry away a vehicle. If you are trapped in floodwater in a car, stay inside. If the inside of the vehicle starts to flood, climb onto the roof.

include in an emergency kit. The site also provides additional disaster preparedness advice.

Important documents and valuables should be secured in waterproof containers. They should be stored well above flood level. Copies of certain documents, such as prescriptions, should be included in the emergency kit.

People should have a communication plan in place in case of disaster. They should sign up for alerts offered in their area. These announcements include NWS alerts as well as specific watches or warnings. Examples include coastal flooding, river flooding, or tsunamis. Local authorities may send out text, phone, and email alerts as well. People should also make arrangements to keep in contact with family and friends during floods or tsunamis. Social media can be very useful for staying in touch. But you should have a backup plan, too.

During a severe flood or tsunami, the local authorities may order residents to evacuate. A voluntary evacuation means that people can

# FLOOD SAFETY TIPS

## BEFORE

STAY INFORMED ON LOCAL NEWS

PREPARE AN EMERGENCY BAG WITH FOOD, DRUGS, DOCUMENTS, FLASHLIGHT, PET ITEMS

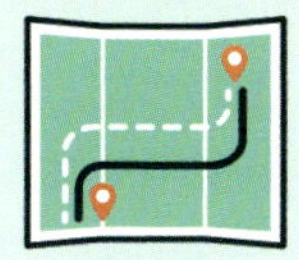

KNOW HOW TO EVACUATE AND SAFE ALTERNATIVE ROUTES

LEAVE BEFORE FLOODING STARTS

IN FLOOD-PRONE AREAS: KEEP USEFUL ITEMS AT HOME (SANDBAGS, LADDER, ROPE...)

## DURING THE FLOOD

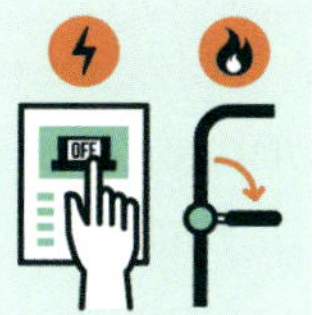


DISCONNECT ELECTRICITY AND GAS

DON'T WALK OR DRIVE IN FLOODWATER

GET TO A HIGHER GROUND

FOLLOW EVACUATION ORDERS

FREE CATTLE AND LEAD ANIMALS TO A SAFER PLACE

## AFTER

AVOID CONTACT WITH FLOODWATER AND SWIMMING

DON'T TOUCH POWER LINES

DON'T GO HOME OR TO DISASTER AREAS UNTIL IT IS DECLARED SAFE

COMMUNICATE TO YOUR FAMILY THAT YOU ARE SAFE

WHEN BACK HOME: CLEAN AND DISINFECT SURFACES AND ITEMS

Flood safety tips for before, during, and after a flood are listed here. Basic emergency preparedness measures can help save lives and minimize property damage.

decide whether or not to leave their homes. A mandatory evacuation means that people must evacuate. People should plan out evacuation routes ahead of time. They should also know where to go for shelter.

People should be aware of dangerous situations as they evacuate. If a tsunami is predicted, you should try to reach high ground as quickly as possible. A tsunami and earthquake may occur at the same time. If the ground shakes, you should drop to the ground, take cover, and hold on to something solid. Bridges can be unsafe during both floods and tsunamis. They are vulnerable to being washed away. Low-lying places such as underground parking garages and underpasses are also dangerous places to be in such an event. They can flood quickly.

Residents should stay out of evacuated areas until the evacuation order is lifted. When it's safe, authorities will allow people to return to their homes.

STEM principles inform every level of flood and tsunami preparedness, from detection by federal agencies down to the recommendations for individual protection and safety. Scientists and engineers develop the instruments that detect and monitor disasters. They design infrastructure and construction methods that can withstand floods and tsunamis. During disasters, people rely on communication systems made possible by STEM innovations. Recommendations by authorities, based on sound science and engineering, keep people safe and mitigate the damage from floods and tsunamis.

# Glossary

**asteroid** A small rocky body that moves around the sun.

**catastrophic** Causing sudden and considerable destruction or suffering.

**climate change** The large-scale change in Earth's weather patterns over a long period of time, marked by rising sea levels, melting snow and ice cover, and extreme weather events.

**contaminate** To make something dirty or impure by adding a substance that pollutes it.

**cyclone** An atmospheric area that has lower pressure than its surrounding areas and winds that rotate toward the center. A hurricane is sometimes called a tropical cyclone.

**debris** Broken remains that are left after something has been destroyed.

**dike** A wall that holds back water, such as in a river or sea.

**evacuate** To leave a home, town, or area because it is not safe.

**floodplain** The low-lying area surrounding a river that is subject to flooding.

**hazard** Something that is dangerous.

**infrastructure** Facilities and systems, such as roads, communication systems, power facilities, and so forth, that are necessary for a country to function.

**innovative** New and original; often technically advanced.

**inundation** Covering over by water.

**landslide** The sliding of rocks and earth down a steep slope.

**levee** An embankment built beside a river to prevent flooding.

**mitigate** To reduce the damage caused by something.

**permeable** Allowing liquids or gases to pass through.

**recede** To go back down or retreat.

**satellite** An artificial or man-made body that orbits Earth and other bodies, often to make observations or transmit communication signals.

**seismic** Pertaining to earthquakes or other vibrations in the earth.

**tectonic plate** One of the slowly moving pieces that make up Earth's crust.

**tide** The regular rise and fall of ocean levels caused by the attraction of the moon and sun.

**tsunami** A series of ocean waves caused by earthquakes or other disturbances.

**vulnerable** Liable to be damaged by a hazard or disaster.

# For More Information

American Red Cross National Headquarters
431 18th Street NW
Washington, DC 20006
(800) 733-2767
Website: https://www.redcross.org
Facebook: @redcross
Instagram: @americanredcross
Twitter: @RedCross
The American Red Cross provides disaster and emergency relief, such as shelter, food, and relief items, to people in need and also assists in helping communities recover and in preventing future disasters.

Federal Emergency Management Agency (FEMA)
500 C Street SW
Washington, DC 20472
(202) 646-2500
Website: https://www.fema.gov
Facebook: @ FEMA
Instagram and Twitter: @fema
The Federal Emergency Management Agency is the government agency that works to prevent disasters and responds to disasters.

Get Prepared
(800) 622-6232
Website: https://www.getprepared.gc.ca/index-eng.aspx
Twitter: @Get_Prepared
The Canadian government's Get Prepared campaign offers

informational resources on how Canadians can prepare for emergencies.

National Oceanic and Atmospheric Administration (NOAA)
1401 Constitution Avenue NW, Room 5128
Washington, DC 20230
Website: https://www.noaa.gov
Facebook and Twitter: @NOAA
Instagram: @noaa
The National Oceanic and Atmospheric Administration studies and informs the public about changes in climate, weather, oceans, and coasts. The National Weather Service (NWS) is part of NOAA.

Public Safety Canada
269 Laurier Avenue West
Ottawa, ON K1A 0P8
Canada
(613) 944-4875
Website: https://www.publicsafety.gc.ca
Twitter: @Safety_Canada
Public Safety Canada is Canada's national security department. Its responsibilities include handling natural disasters and emergency management.

Ready.gov
Ready Campaign
FEMA/DHS
500 C Street SW
Washington, DC 20472
(800) 621-3362
Website: https://www.ready.gov
Facebook: @readygov

Twitter: @Readygov
Ready.gov provides Americans and their communities with disaster preparedness resources. The website includes web pages for young people on floods and tsunamis and other natural disasters.

US Army Corps of Engineers
Headquarters
441 G Street NW
Washington, DC 20314-1000
Website: https://www.usace.army.mil
Facebook and Twitter: @USACEHQ
The US Army Corps of Engineers provides engineering services that include disaster response and prevention projects.

US Geological Survey (USGS)
US Geological Survey Headquarters
12201 Sunrise Valley Drive
Reston, VA 20192
Website: https://www.usgs.gov
Facebook: @USGeologicalSurvey
Instagram: @usgs
Twitter: @USGS
The US Geological Survey is the government agency that provides expertise on the country's natural resources and natural hazards.

# For Further Reading


Chambers, Catherine. *Can We Protect People from Natural Disasters?* Chicago, IL: Capstone Heinemann Library, 2015.

Cosgrove, Brian. *Weather: Discover the World's Weather from Heat Waves and Droughts to Blizzards and Floods.* New York, NY: DK Publishing, 2016.

Cummings, Judy Dodge. *Earth, Wind, Fire, and Rain: Real Tales of Temperamental Elements.* White River Junction, VT: Nomad Press, 2018.

Koontz, Robin Michal. *Disaster-Proof!* (Define & Design). North Mankato, MN: Rourke Educational Media, 2018.

Koontz, Robin Michal. *The Science of a Tsunami.* Ann Arbor, MI: Cherry Lake Publishing, 2016.

Kostigen, Thomas. *Extreme Weather.* Washington, DC: National Geographic, 2014.

Marquardt, Meg. *The Science of a Flood.* Ann Arbor, MI: Cherry Lake Publishing, 2016.

Raum, Elizabeth. *Flood!* Mankato, MN: Amicus, 2017.

Rissman, Rebecca. *Swept Away.* North Mankato, MN: Capstone Press, 2017.

Roker, Al. *Al Roker's Extreme Weather.* New York, NY: Harper, 2017.

Squire, Ann. *Tsunamis*. New York, NY: Scholastic, 2016.

Watts, Claire. *Natural Disasters.* New York, NY: DK Publishing, 2015.

# Bibliography

Baggaley, Kate. "How to Survive a Tsunami. *Popular Science*, June 27, 2017. https://www.popsci.com/what-to-do-tsunami-survival.

Becker, Rachel. "Japan's Tsunami Warning System Worked Well in Today's Major Earthquake." The Verge, November 21, 2016. https://www.theverge.com/2016/11/21/13710204/japan-earthquake-tsunami-fukushima-daini-nuclear-plant-2016.

Demetriou, Danielle. "Tsunami Two Years On: Japan Finally Gets Warning System That Would Have Saved Hundreds of Lives." *Telegraph*, March 9, 2013. https://www.telegraph.co.uk/news/worldnews/asia/japan/9920042/Tsunami-two-years-on-Japan-finally-gets-warning-system-that-would-have-saved-hundreds-of-lives.html.

Environmental Protection Agency. "Green Infrastructure: Manage Flood Risk." September 14, 2016. https://www.epa.gov/green-infrastructure/manage-flood-risk.

Exploring Earth. "Have Flood Controls on the Mississippi River Been Successful?" Introduction from Exploring Earth website, McDougal Littell. Retrieved February 11, 2019. https://www.classzone.com/books/earth_science/terc/content/investigations/es1308/es1308page01.cfm?chapter_no=investigation.

Federal Emergency Management Agency (FEMA). "Flood After Fire." September 14, 2018. https://www.fema.gov/flood-after-fire.

Federal Emergency Management Agency (FEMA). "Mitigation Ideas: A Resource for Reducing Risk to Natural Hazards." January 2013. https://www.fema.gov/media-library/assets/documents/30627.

Federal Emergency Management Agency (FEMA). "National Tsunami Hazard Mitigation Program: Preparing for Tsunami Hazards." July 19, 2016. https://www.fema.gov/media-library/assets/documents/5949.

Flechas, Joey. "Miami Beach to Begin New $100 Million Flood Prevention Project in Face of Sea Level Rise." *Miami Herald*, January 28, 2017. https://www.miamiherald.com/news/local/community/miami-dade/miami-beach/article129284119.html.

Freemantle, Tony. "In Harvey's Wake, Dutch Have Much to Teach Houston." *Houston Chronicle*, December 22, 2017. https://www.houstonchronicle.com/news/houston-texas/houston/article/In-Harvey-s-wake-Dutch-have-much-to-teach-Houston-12445243.php.

Ghose, Tia. "Are Ocean Asteroid Impacts Really a Serious Threat?" LiveScience, December 31, 2014. https://www.livescience.com/49298-asteroids-causing-tsunamis.html.

Holmes, Robert R., Jr. "The 100-Year Flood—It's All About Chance." US Geological Survey, December 7, 2017. https://water.usgs.gov/edu/100yearflood-basic.html.

Iovenko, Chris. "Dutch Masters: The Netherlands Exports Flood-Control Expertise." *EARTH Magazine*, October 15, 2018. https://www.earthmagazine.org/article/dutch-masters-netherlands-exports-flood-control-expertise.

Knight, Sophie. "What Would an Entirely Flood-Proof City Look Like?" *Guardian*, September 25, 2017. https://www.theguardian.com/cities/2017/sep/25/what-flood-proof-city-china-dhaka-houston.

Komatsu, Matthew. "Preparing for Japan's Next Tsunami." Motherboard, August 25, 2018. https://motherboard.vice.com/en_us/article/d3e5av/japan-tsunami-alert-system.

Kusky, Timothy. *Tsunamis: Giant Waves from the Sea.* New York, NY: Facts On File, 2008.

Lim, Megumi. "Seven Years After Tsunami, Japanese Live Uneasily with Seawalls." Reuters, March 8, 2018. https://www.reuters

.com/article/us-japan-disaster-seawalls/seven-years-after-tsunami-japanese-live-uneasily-with-seawalls-idUSKCN1GL0DK.

Lohmann, Patrick. "Flood That Hit Boy Scouts May Have Reached 20 Feet." *Albuquerque Journal*, June 29, 2015. https://www.abqjournal.com/605774/flood-that-hit-boy-scouts-may-have-reached-20-feet.html.

*Los Angeles Times*. "Rebuild Paradise? California Has to Reconsider Putting Homes in the Path of More Dangerous Fires." Editorial, November 24, 2018. https://www.latimes.com/opinion/editorials/la-ed-wildfire-rebuild-20181124-story.html.

Milman, Oliver. "Climate Change Is Making Hurricanes Even More Destructive, Research Finds." *Guardian*, November 14, 2018. https://www.theguardian.com/environment/2018/nov/14/climate-change-hurricanes-study-global-warming.

National Conference of State Legislatures. "Flood Mitigation." September 12, 2018. http://www.ncsl.org/research/environment-and-natural-resources/flood-mitigation.aspx.

National Oceanic and Atmospheric Administration (NOAA). "Tsunamis." October 2018. https://www.noaa.gov/education/resource-collections/ocean-coasts-education-resources/tsunamis.

National Oceanic and Atmospheric Administration (NOAA). "U.S. Tsunami Warning System." September 29, 2017. https://www.noaa.gov/explainers/us-tsunami-warning-system.

National Ocean Service. "What Percentage of the American Population Lives Near the Coast?" June 25, 2018. https://oceanservice.noaa.gov/facts/population.html.

National Research Council of the National Academies Press. *Levees and the National Flood Insurance Program: Improving Policies and Practices*. Washington, DC: The National Academies Press, 2013. https://www.nap.edu/read/18309/chapter/1.

National Severe Storms Laboratory. "Severe Weather 101: Flood Basics." Retrieved February 11, 2019. https://www.nssl.noaa.gov/education/svrwx101/floods.

National Weather Service. "About Tsunamis." Retrieved February 11, 2019. https://www.weather.gov/safety/tsunami-about.

National Weather Service. "Flood Safety Tips and Resources." Retrieved February 11, 2019. https://www.weather.gov/safety/flood.

NOAA/National Weather Service. "Tsunami Frequently Asked Questions." February 7, 2019. https://tsunami.gov/?page=tsunamiFAQ.

Office of Communications and Publishing. "Indian Ocean Tsunami Remembered—Scientists Reflect on the 2004 Indian Ocean That Killed Thousands." US Geological Survey, December 23, 2014. https://www.usgs.gov/news/indian-ocean-tsunami-remembered-scientists-reflect-2004-indian-ocean-killed-thousands.

Oskin, Becky. "Japan Earthquake & Tsunami of 2011: Facts and Information." LiveScience, September 13, 2017. https://www.livescience.com/39110-japan-2011-earthquake-tsunami-facts.html.

Rahman, Fauzeya. "Houston City Council Passes New Floodplain Building Restrictions." *Houston Business Journal*, April 4, 2018. https://www.bizjournals.com/houston/news/2018/04/04/houstoncity-council-passes-new-floodplain-building.html.

Rauhala, Emily. "How Japan Became a Leader in Disaster Preparation." *Time*, March 11, 2011. http://content.time.com/time/world/article/0,8599,2058390,00.html.

Ready.gov. "Floods." Retrieved February 11, 2019. https://www.ready.gov/floods.

Ready.gov. "Tsunamis." Retrieved February 11, 2019. https://www.ready.gov/tsunamis.

Reid, Kathryn. "2011 Japan Earthquake and Tsunami." World Vision, May 7, 2018. https://www.worldvision.org/disaster-relief-news-stories/2011-japan-earthquake-and-tsunami-facts.

US Army Corps of Engineers. "MR&T Post Flood Report." Retrieved February 11, 2019. https://www.mvd.usace.army.mil/Missions/Flood-Risk-Management/Regional-Flood-Risk-Management-Program/MR-T-Post-Flood-Report.

US Geological Survey. "Tsunami Hazards—A National Threat." February 2006. https://pubs.usgs.gov/fs/2006/3023/2006-3023.pdf.

Wax-Thibodeaux, Emily, et al. "Houston Dam Spills Over for the First Time in History, Overwhelmed by Harvey Rainfall." *Washington Post,* August 29, 2017. https://www.washingtonpost.com/news/post-nation/wp/2017/08/28/houston-releases-water-from-two-dams-in-attempt-to-prevent-uncontrolled-overflow.

Webley, Kayla. "Top 10 Historic U.S. Floods." *Time*, May 11, 2011. http://content.time.com/time/specials/packages/article/0,28804,2070796_2070798_2070780,00.html.

Withington, John. *Flood: Nature and Culture*. London, UK: Reaktion Books, 2013.

Zirker, J. B. *The Science of Ocean Waves: Ripples, Tsunamis and Stormy Seas*. Baltimore, MD: The Johns Hopkins University Press, 2013.

# Index

# About the Author

Corona Brezina has written numerous books for young adults. Several of her previous works have also focused on topics related to science and technology, including *Careers in Meteorology*, *Einstein and Relativity*, *Time Travel*, and *Artificial Intelligence and You*. She lives in Chicago, Illinois.

# Photo Credits

Cover Edwin Remsberg/Photolibrary/Getty Images; cover hexagons (left to right) Nattapong Wongloungud/EyeEm/Getty Images, CHUYN/E+/Getty Images, D-Keine/E+/Getty Images, © iStockphoto.com/Alessandro Rizzo, john finney photography/Moment/Getty Images, Fernando Ojeda/EyeEm/Getty Images; pp. 4-5 (background) Warchi/iStock/Getty Images; p. 5 (inset) Mario Tama/Getty Images; p. 7 The Asahi Shimbun/Getty Images; p. 8 Erich Schlegel/Getty Images; p. 11 Doroniuk Anastasiia/Shutterstock.com; p. 13 NASA; p. 15 Baltimore Sun/Tribune News Service/Getty Images; p. 16 Bloomberg/Getty Images; p. 19 Studio BKK/Shutterstock.com; p. 22 Ramin Talaie/Getty Images; p. 23 picture alliance/Getty Images; p. 25 Paul J. Richards/AFP/Getty Images; p. 26 MediaNews Group/Orange County Register/Getty Images; p. 28 frans lemmens/Alamy Stock Photo; p. 31 Andrew Burton/Getty Images; p. 33 elenabsl/Shutterstock.com; cover and interior pages graphic elements © iStockphoto.com/koto_feja (spiral design), Ralf Hiemisch/Getty Images (dot pattern).

Design and Layout: Tahara Anderson; Senior Editor: Kathy Kuhtz Campbell; Photo Researcher: Sherri Jackson.